THE MEDITERRANEAN COOKBOOK

Eat, Drink & Live Well with 70+ Mouth-Watering Recipes to Improve Your Lifestyle & Shred Away Those Extra Pounds.

Bianca DeVille

©Copyright 2018 by Cascade Publishing

All rights reserved.

It is not legal to reproduce, duplicate, or transmit any part of this document in either electronic means or in printed format. Recording of this publication is strictly prohibited.

CONTENTS

INTRODUCTION 1
Chapter One The Mediterranean Diet 3
    The Roots of the Mediterranean Diet 3
    The Staple Food of the Mediterranean Diet 3
    The Use of Herbs and Spices 4
    Why It Works 5
Chapter Two The Key Components of the Mediterranean Diet 6
    Food to Eat and Food to Avoid 7
    Food Groups to Avoid 8
    The Notable Benefits of Olive Oil 8
    Why Olive Oil is Good for the Body 9
    Is Olive Oil Effective for Weight Loss? 11
    Portion Control 11
Chapter Three The Health Benefits of the Mediterranean Diet 12
    THE MEDITERRANEAN DIET FOOD PYRAMID! 14
    Mediterranean Food Shopping list 18
Chapter Four Breakfast Recipes 21
    Morning Sweet Potato Scramble 21
    Eggplant and Lamb Omelet 23
    Raisins, Seeds, and Nuts Granola 25
    Ground Chicken and Avocado Scramble 26
    Cheesy Tofu Quiche 27
    Breakfast Jalapeno Tofu Mix 28
    Mushroom Soup with Red Wine 29
    Pita Chicken Burger 31
    Green Beans Salad in Red Wine Vinegar 32
    Olives and Cheese 33
    Berry and Maple Pancakes 34
    Paprika Eggs 35
    Sardines and Greens Salad 36
    Mediterranean Muesli 37
    Vegetarian Morning Crepes 38

Eggplant and Garlic Salad 39
Pumpkin Dark Choco Muffins 40
Pumpkin Cilantro Soup 41
Chapter Five Lunch Recipes 42
Moroccan Tomato Soup 42
Grilled Salmon with Avocado Salsa 44
Green Lentils and Mixed Vegetables Soup 45
Okra in Red Wine Vinegar 46
Lamb Saffron Stew 48
Tuna, Tomato, and Red Pepper Tortilla 50
Grilled Pita with Chickpea 51
Lamb in Tomato Sauce and White Wine 52
Duck Legs with Chickpeas and Olives 54
Curry Squash and Apple Soup 56
Arugula, Cherry Tomatoes, and Artichoke Salad 58
Octopus with Frisée and Capers 59
Roasted Stuffed Snapper 61
Ground Beef and Tomato Stuffed Eggplant 63
Chickpea and Brown Rice Patties with Salsa 65
Chapter Six Snacks 67
Feta Nibbles with Poppy Seeds 67
Cabbage and Cheese Sandwich 69
Gingerbread Waffles 70
Flax Rice Bran Bread 71
Avocado and Carrot Muffins 72
Cold Beans and Olives Salad 73
Peaches and Cream Muffins 74
Wheat Lentil Tortillas 75
All Vegetables Tacos 76
Minty Greek Yogurt with Fruits and Nuts 77
Prosciutto and Figs Wrap 78
Dark Choco Flavored Zucchini Muffins 79
Honey Onion Biscuits 81
Butter Pecan Munchies 82
Blueberry Pie 83
Butter and Soy Pecans 84

Veggie Burrito Wheat Wrap 85
Chapter Seven Dinner **86**
　　Italian Tuna Fillets with Raisins 86
　　Cheesy and Creamy Cauliflower Salad 88
　　Shrimp and Tomato Pasta 89
　　Honey Chicken Glaze 90
　　Kelp Curry Noodles 91
　　Teriyaki Chicken Salad 93
　　Lamb and Beef Meatballs 95
　　Garlic Broccoli 96
　　Shrimp with Romesco Sauce 97
　　Red Peppers Stuffed Rice and Mushrooms 99
　　Baked Aioli Fish Fillets 101
　　Greek All Veggie Salad 102
　　Bake Meatballs Stew 104
Chapter Eight Desserts **106**
　　Cinnamon Sweet Potato Biscuits 106
　　Honey Chives Biscuits 108
　　Apple and Cranberry Crumble 109
　　Brown Rice, Almonds, and Raisins Pudding 111
　　Cinnamon Dark Choco Oatmeal Bars 112
　　Cheesy Olives and Rosemary Topping 114
　　Banana Oats Muffins 115
　　Almond and Apricot Cookies 116
　　Almond and Cacao Bites 117
　　Dates and Walnuts Nibbles 119
Conclusion **120**

INTRODUCTION

This book contains established steps and strategies on how to lose weight, eat clean and healthy food, and improve your overall health by following the Mediterranean diet. The main principles behind the Mediterranean diet comprise of 2 things: enjoy fresh food and eat with the people who matter to you the most.

The history of this diet can be traced back to the lifestyle of the natives of Southern Italy. During the 1960's, many scientists were led to conduct a research concerning the diet of the natives of the Mediterranean regions. In the year 2010, the Mediterranean diet was officially declared by the UNESCO as a part of the cultural heritage of Italy, Greece, Spain, and Morocco.

Indeed, the Mediterranean diet represents healthy living and celebrates good food. It goes beyond giving you short term weight loss and exceeds to refining your physical and mental health.

This book is rich with information regarding the following:

- Mediterranean diet and its key ingredients
- How the Mediterranean diet works

- Key components and how you can apply this diet to lose weight
- What to eat and what not to eat
- Delicious and easy-to-prepare recipes

Most important of all, the diet is all about enjoying life. It embraces healthy and delicious food and considers eating alone to be unhealthy. As often as you can, enjoy your meals with a companion and savor each bite the Mediterranean way.

Chapter One

The Mediterranean Diet

The Roots of the Mediterranean Diet

The main source of this diet comes from the kind of lifestyle the locals near the Mediterranean Sea led. Summertime in the areas surrounding the Mediterranean is typically hot, while wintertime brings in rains. The land itself is mostly rocky, which promoted the cultivation of grapes, olives, and other fruits. Its close proximity to the Mediterranean Sea has led to an abundance of fish and other seafood. There are also the pastoralism of sheep, chicken, and goats. Thus, the food of the natives in the Mediterranean region are different from that of the traditional Western lifestyle, which is mainly consisted of pork and beef. The Mediterranean diet is a buffet of fresh fruits and vegetables, healthy fats, lean protein, and seafood.

The Staple Food of the Mediterranean Diet

A great significance is put on the consumption of plant food in this diet because they are low in calories but still provides important vitamins and minerals. These are rich, low-calorie sources of a wide array of nutrients. Those who follow the Mediterranean diet consume roughly 8 servings of fruits and vegetables in a day, and they make an effort to incorporate at least 2-3 servings of vegetables in every meal.

Here's a list of staple food that are grown locally in the Mediterranean regions:

- ✓ Grains including rice, wheat, corn, and barley.
- ✓ Vegetables consisting of broccoli, eggplant, asparagus, tomato, cabbage, artichokes, garlic, onion, and green beans.
- ✓ Fruits such as olive, grapes, lemon, fig, persimmons, mandarin orange, and pomegranate
- ✓ Legumes including peas, chickpeas, and lentils
- ✓ Nuts such as walnut, almond, pine nut, and hazelnut

The Use of Herbs and Spices

In the Mediterranean, people make use of fresh and dried herbs and spices for their dishes. Each herb and spice is rich in antioxidants that help fight cancers, and omega-3 fatty acids that lessen disease-causing inflammation. All of which offer amazing and a wide array of health benefits. Some of the most common herbs and spices used in many Mediterranean recipes are oregano, rosemary, basil, cinnamon, dill, mint, parsley, sage and thyme.

When it comes to physical activities, the locals of the Mediterranean regions value this so much. They are into an active lifestyle and believe that exercise should be part of one's everyday life. As for social relationships, the Mediterranean culture places greater emphasis on community. Eating alone is considered unhealthy. Therefore, they always make it a point to have at least one meal with family or friends. A healthy social relationship reduces stress, and spending time with your loved ones during meal time is one way of being socially healthy.

Why It Works

The Mediterranean diet works for weight loss because it is realistic and holistic. Each meal under this diet is enjoyable, affordable, and non-restrictive.

There are many kinds of diets that have reached the mainstream level, but none can parallel to the weight loss benefits that can be derived from the Mediterranean diet. This diet is notable in that it proves to be the one with a great number of studies conducted.

According to medical studies, the Mediterranean diet can help decrease the chances of mortality. This diet has high levels of dietary fiber and monounsaturated fats, and has very low levels of saturated fat. The inclusion of olive oil is one of the main reasons why it is a highly recommended diet.

This diet works because it is served in small yet filling portions that can be consumed more frequently. There is emphasis on balance and pleasure in the kind of lifestyle the locals lead. This diet also serves food that are both pleasurable to the taste buds and beneficial for one's health.

The components connected to the dietary aspects are one of the many reasons why people in the Mediterranean cultures are leading healthier lifestyles. One can never really underestimate the benefits of having regular physical activities and a balance nutritional intake.

Chapter Two

The Key Components of the Mediterranean Diet

There are specific food groups that should be taken in specific amounts. The following are the ones that should be included in your diet:

1. Grains, fruits, and vegetables - Mediterranean countries often have vegetables, fruits, and rice included in their diet. For instance, Greek people eat small amounts of red meat because their diet is consisted mainly of vegetables and fruits known to be rich in antioxidants. This kind of diet assists in lowering down the level of oxidation of low-density lipoprotein (LDL), known as the "bad" cholesterol. LDL cholesterol blocks the arteries and veins that often lead to serious heart problems.
2. Dairy, poultry, and fish – with moderation, there is nothing wrong in eating dairy, poultry, and fish products even if they're high in calories. According to AHA or the

American Heart Association, the fat contained in these food groups are classified as monounsaturated and help protect against different heart diseases. They also boost one's overall immune system functions.

3. Healthy fat - The focus of the Mediterranean diet is on the consumption of good, healthy fats that contain linolenic acid. This is a kind of omega-3 fatty acid that provides favorable effects to the body. Some examples of healthy fats are olive oil and nuts.

4. Wine – yes, consumption of alcohol is highly recommended in the Mediterranean diet as long as it is kept in moderate amounts. Drinking in proper proportion is beneficial and can reduce the risk of heart ailment. Take for example red wine. This has antioxidant properties that can lessen the risk of having cancer and lowers the clotting level. According to the Mediterranean diet, those over the age of 65 are encouraged to consume 5 ounces of wine on a daily basis. On the other hand, those who are under the specified age can take 10 ounces of wine daily.

5. Up your workout and water intake – A regular exercise that can strengthen the cardiovascular system is important. The diet recommends regular physical exercises such as walking, jogging, or aerobics. Similarly, drinking six to eight glasses of water every day is advised to keep your weight down.

Food to Eat and Food to Avoid

The biggest portion in any meal should be allotted to vegetables, especially leafy greens that are low in calories and high in nutrient and fiber content. In fact, the locals eat at least 5 servings of vegetables and fruits every day. Simply put, you eat until you are full without gaining a lot of weight due to the low caloric nutrition.

Another staple of the Mediterranean Diet is seafood, which is considered to be rich protein and low in calories. The recommended intake is at least twice a week. The diet favors fish, shrimp, mussels, scallops, and other seafood.

Eggs, chicken, cheese, turkey, and yogurt are also staples in the diet, although you should eat them in moderation.

Spices and herbs add flavor to one's meals and are allowed in this diet. Better stock up on turmeric, basil, parsley, cumin, oregano, and cinnamon.

Food Groups to Avoid

The diet discourages regular consumption of:

- ❖ Sweets
- ❖ Desserts
- ❖ Processed meats
- ❖ Red meat
- ❖ Excessive use of sugar and salt

If you can't stop yourself from eating these, it is advised that you eat in small portions once a week.

The Notable Benefits of Olive Oil

The Mediterranean diet will not be what it is without olive oil. Olives are locally grown in the Mediterranean and can be considered as a healthy alternative to the Western diet's hydrogenated oils.

Did you know that 1 tablespoon of olive oil is 14 grams of fat or 120 calories? This is why it is still advised that this be used sparingly. The great news is that olive oil contains healthy fats full of monounsaturated fatty acids that help in weight loss and improve heart health.

Olive oil also comprises of the following nutrients: Vitamin E - helps improve the immune system, Vitamin K - helps the body absorb calcium more efficiently, promotes blood clotting, and improves blood vessel condition, Lutein, Beta-carotene, and Zeaxanthin, all of which are fat-soluble carotenoids that keep the arteries, eyes, and overall immune system healthy. Hydroytryosol, Tyrosol, and other Polyphenols that are antioxidants, which aid in minimizing inflammation and lower both blood pressure and cholesterol levels), and Chlorophyll (which also has antioxidant benefits and is the biochemical that gives olive oil its greenish color).

Why Olive Oil is Good for the Body

Olive oil is definitely worth the price. Here is a list of amazing health benefits that it can do for the body:

1. *Olive oil boosts memory and cognition.* According to studies, consuming 2-3 tablespoons of olive oil each day lowers the risk of acquiring cognition problems. This is due mainly to "oleocanthal", a compound that improves nerve cell damage.

2. *Olive oil stabilizes cholesterol levels.* The "bad" cholesterol also known as LDL cholesterol is significantly lowered when regularly used for cooking meals, while good cholesterol or HDL cholesterol is raised. This lowers the risk of developing heart diseases or reverse them.

3. *Olive oil lessens inflammation.* The oleocanthal compound aids in blocking the inflammatory process that is activated by certain enzymes. Think of it as a version of the medication ibuprofen, only this one is all-natural.

4. *Olive oil reduces the outcomes of oxidative stress.* Oxidation is the process responsible for accumulating plaque in the arteries leading to a risk for grave cardiovascular diseases, heart attack, and stroke.

5. *Olive oil controls blood glucose levels.* Regular consumption of olive oil is more favorable for people with diabetes because it helps in controlling their blood glucose levels.

6. *Olive oil enhances nutrient absorption and boosts digestive system.* Olive oil aids in the absorption of essential nutrients from the food you eat.

7. *Olive oil lowers the risks of developing cancer.* According to studies, those who include olive oil in their regular diet displayed a reduced risk of cancer, particularly breast cancer. Olive oil contains oleic acid that stops the type of protein responsible for the development of cancer cells.

8. *Olive oil helps prevent osteoporosis.* It contains vitamin K that makes it easier for the cells to absorb calcium. This is why olive oil is often linked to bone health.

9. *Olive oil prevents stomach issues.* Those who suffer from stomach ulcers will benefit from olive oil polyphenols as these prevent the growth of *H. pylori*. This is a type of bacteria that mainly causes stomach cancer.

Is Olive Oil Effective for Weight Loss?

It may sound ironic to think that olive oil can make you lose weight. However, the reason is simple, it is only through the Mediterranean diet or some carful planning that you can acquire the weight loss benefits of olive oil. Pairing the oil with an existing diet rich in animal protein, simple carbohydrates, and sugar will only make you gain weight without careful consideration.

Introducing olive oil into the Mediterranean diet has proven to be effective because the healthy fats in this diet lowers the risk of heart diseases based on several studies. In particular, a group of participants who consumed 4 tablespoons of extra virgin olive oil each day as part of their Mediterranean diet showed 25 to 30 percent drop of suffering from stroke or heart attack.

Portion Control

As always, everything must be consumed in moderation. Yes, olive oil has many health and weight loss benefits, but it does not mean that you should gulp a bottleful each day. In order to control how much olive oil you allot into your Mediterranean meals each day, refer to the information below:

- Daily Caloric Limit: 1,500 - Olive oil: 2 tablespoons
- Daily Caloric Limit: 1,800 - Olive oil: 2 to 3 tablespoons
- Daily Caloric Limit: 2,100 - Olive oil: 3 tablespoons
- Daily Caloric Limit: 2,400 - Olive oil 3 to 4 tablespoons

Remember to measure the amount of olive oil that you consume each day based on your daily caloric limit. Anything more than the recommended amount will work against your weight loss goals.

Chapter Three

The Health Benefits of the Mediterranean Diet

The factors that highly contribute to the impressive performance of the Mediterranean diet are known from the benefits one can get from said diet. People in the Mediterranean are aware of the medical benefits that a healthy lifestyle can bring.

In a study conducted by the Journal of American Medical Association, it was discovered that following the Mediterranean diet can cut down the risk of early death to as much as 50 percent. Also, the risk of having Type II Diabetes and Alzheimer's disease are said to be significantly cut down.

According to medical research, the presence of fats in the Mediterranean diet have a strong purpose. These help in the promotion of the atheroprotective properties of the diet that cannot be supported by olive oil alone.

The Mediterranean diet can also aid in protecting you from acquiring skin cancer.

The vitamin C components from fruits and healthy oils in the Mediterranean diet are said to reduce mortality rate by as much as 70 percent.

Adhering to the Mediterranean diet in the strictest sense can save a person's life. The level of probability to acquire cardiovascular diseases and different types of cancers is greatly reduced. People who are following the diet are less likely to acquire Parkinson's and Alzheimer's diseases.

The higher the level of consumption of vegetables and the lower consumption of meat reduce the level of risk and mortality. Mortality is also found to be significantly reduced by the following: high level of consumption of legumes, nuts, and fruits. There should also be moderate intake of alcohol.

The eating style promoted by the Mediterranean diet does not only promote weight management, but also proves to be significant in prolonging one's life.

The Mediterranean diet proves to be a relevant paradigm for the propagation of healthy kind of living.

The Mediterranean Diet Food Pyramid!

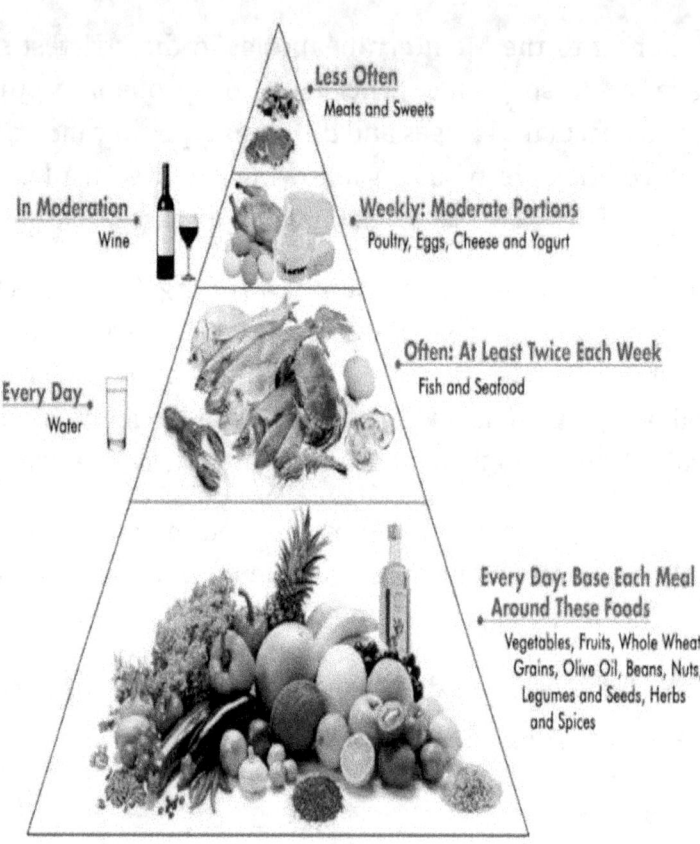

The Mediterranean diet is consists of five major groups, four of which are food. The most significant and a big chunk of the pyramid belongs to being active, spending quality time with your loved ones, and enjoying life. To the Mediterranean people, eating alone is very unhealthy and works against your mental well-being.

The second most important group includes vegetables, fruits, and grains. This also includes olive oil, herbs and spices.

The third group encourages to eat fish and other seafood at least twice a week. Also, making sure to drink plenty of water.

The fourth consists of poultry, eggs, yogurt, and cheese. It is best that you stock up on more cheese for this diet.

The last section consists of meats such as pork, beef, and lamb. Consume a serving of these meats only once or twice a week. This also goes for sweets. In Western countries, these are the most frequently consumed food, which may be the main reason why diseases such as strokes, high blood, high cholesterol, and type 2 diabetes are so common.

The Mediterranean diet gives you more reason to live a healthier life. It does not only put emphasis on the modification of your dietary patterns, but also requires a holistic change in one's lifestyle. And, to make sure that you reap the rewards of this diet, you must consider maintaining and strictly adhering to this diet for good.

According to many health studies, sustained and maintained weight loss can be achieved only if you have the will power to continue following the guidelines no matter the circumstances. Skipping your workouts or cheating on your diet only sets you back further away from your goal. Remember this is not a competition, you are trying to to work towards a lifestyle change. The best part of this diet is that you are still allowed to eat those yummy foods including pasta, rice, legumes, fresh fruits and vegetables, poultry, dairy, and seafood.

The Mediterranean diet offers a well-balanced variety of meals that promotes long-term health and balanced nutrition. All you have to do is just be aware of the basic components of the diet, from there you can make your own menu/meal plan. Do not stress if you're eating out, just make sure that you go for seafood or fish for your main dish cooked either steamed, roasted, or fried in olive oil for the best results. If the diet is too strict it is highly unlikely that you will stick to it, so take note to try your best and remember this is not a fad diet but a change of lifestyle.

The Mediterranean diet is actually a promise of having a healthier and longer life if properly maintained. In order to maintain your diet, you must take note of the following:

1. Eat clean. This is why majority of your meals must be comprised of plant components (fruits and vegetables). Plant foods are filling and are excellent sources of fiber and phytochemicals. The Mediterranean vegetables include eggplants, zucchini, tomatoes, and bell peppers among others.

2. Make your food more appetizing by using more herbs and spices like onion, garlic, thyme, basil, and oregano.

3. Include grains like couscous, polenta, and bulgur into your diet. This will be additional carbohydrate sources apart from pasta, bread, and cereals.

4. Where applicable always choose fresh. Growing your own vegetables and fruits are also highly recommended.

5. For an alternative protein source, consider fish and seafood.
6. In cooking, make sure healthy fats and oils are used.
7. If you're eating out, your dessert should include fresh fruits, preserved or dried fruits. Other sweets should be eaten only a few times in a week.
8. Have some wine but make sure you drink it in moderate amounts.

Mediterranean Food Shopping list

Vegetables

- Onions
- Garlic
- Green Beans
- Peppers
- Cucumber
- Tomatoes
- Spinach
- Mushrooms
- Romaine Lettuce
- Cabbage
- Okra
- Eggplant
- Celery
- Beets
- Zucchini
- Potatoes
- Broccoli
- Celery
- Carrots

Fruits

- Apricot
- Tangerine
- Apple
- Orange
- Watermelon
- Figs
- Cherries

- Lemon
- Peach
- Cantaloupe
- Pear

Meat and Poultry

- Pork
- Veal
- Chicken
- Ground Beef

Grains

- Whole grain
- Pasta
- Bulgur
- Rice
- Couscous

Fish and Seafood

- Sardines
- Calamari
- Salmon
- Anchovies
- Cod
- Octopus

Beans

- Chickpeas
- Lentils
- White Beans

Dairy

- Feta Cheese
- Mozzarella
- Ricotta
- Yogurt
- Parmesan

Fats and Nuts

- Extra Virgin Olive Oil
- Almonds
- Pine Nuts
- Pistachios
- Tahini
- Sesame Seeds

Herbs and Spices

- Parsley
- Cumin
- Dill
- Oregano
- Cinnamon
- All Spice
- Sea Salt
- Mint
- Basil

Chapter Four

Breakfast Recipes

Morning Sweet Potato Scramble

Ingredients:

- 3 sweet potatoes, peeled, sliced into thin strips
- 4 eggs, beaten
- 1/8 cup fresh cilantro, chopped
- Paprika
- 1 cup olive oil
- Sea salt
- Ground black pepper

Directions:

1. Place a skillet over medium high flame and heat the oil.
2. Add a dash of salt; once sizzling, add the sweet potatoes and cook for 5 minutes, or until golden brown.

3. Drain the fries on paper towels and season with salt and paprika.

4. Remove the oil from the skillet except for about 1/2 tablespoon. Put the drained sweet potatoes back into the skillet and pour the beaten eggs over them.

5. Season with salt and pepper, then once partially set, carefully flip the omelet using a flat spatula. Cook for 8 minutes, or until fully set.

6. Transfer the omelet onto a plate and sprinkle the cilantro on top. Slice in half and serve immediately.

Eggplant and Lamb Omelet

Ingredients:

- 2 eggplant, cut into cubes
- 4 eggs
- 1/4 cup onion, chopped
- 1 garlic clove, minced
- 1/4 lb. ground lean lamb
- 1 Tbsp. tomato paste
- 1/4 cup flat-leaf parsley, finely chopped
- 1/2 tsp. ground coriander
- 1/4 tsp. ground cumin
- Sea salt
- Ground black pepper
- 1 Tbsp. water
- 1/2 Tbsp. olive oil

Directions:

1. Place a non-stick skillet over medium heat and add the olive oil. Let heat before adding the onions. Sauté for 4 minutes or until onions become translucent. Add the salted eggplant cubes and sauté until eggplant becomes tender and lightly browned. Use a slotted spoon to transfer the eggplant and onion mixture onto a plate. Set aside.

2. Place the eggplant cubes in a colander and season with salt. Set aside for an hour. Rinse and pat dry.

3. Using the same skillet, cook the ground lamb over medium heat until browned. Combine the tomato paste and water in a small bowl.

4. Pour this into the ground lamb along with the garlic. Season with salt and black pepper. Reduce heat and cook for 20 minutes or until lamb is well done.

5. Meanwhile, whisk the eggs with the cumin, parsley, and coriander in a bowl. Season with salt and black pepper and beat well to combine.

6. Remove as much fat from the cooked lamb as possible. Then add the eggplant and onion mixture into the skillet and stir to combine.

7. Pour the egg mixture into the skillet and tilt to distribute it evenly. Reduce heat and cook, covered, for 12 minutes or until eggs become fluffy. Remove from the heat and transfer to a plate. Slice into three sections and serve.

Raisins, Seeds, and Nuts Granola

Ingredients:

- ½ cup raisins
- 2 Tbsp. wheat germ
- 1 cup rolled oats
- 2 ½ Tbsp. pumpkin seeds
- 2 ½ Tbsp. walnuts
- 2 ½ Tbsp. sunflower seeds
- 2 ½ Tbsp. coconut flakes
- ¾ tsp cinnamon
- 2 ½ Tbsp. maple syrup

Directions:

1. Set the oven to 325 degrees F.
2. Combine all ingredients, except the maple syrup and raisins, in a bowl.
3. Fold in the maple syrup and mix well. Spread on a baking sheet.
4. Bake for 12 to 15 minutes, stirring once every 3 minutes.
5. Sprinkle in the raisins. Bake for an additional 3 minutes.
6. Set on a cooling rack for 1 hour. Transfer to an airtight container.

Ground Chicken and Avocado Scramble

Ingredients:

- 3 oz ground chicken
- 2 eggs, beaten
- 1/2 avocado, sliced
- 1/4 tsp. olive oil
- 1/2 cup cherry tomatoes, halved
- 2 cups packed spinach
- 1/8 cup sliced black olives
- 1/8 tsp. fine sea salt
- 1/8 tsp freshly ground black pepper
- 1 Tbsp. fresh cilantro, chopped

Directions:

1. Place a skillet over medium flame and lightly grease with olive oil. Sauté the ground meat and season with salt and pepper. Cook for 4 minutes or until browned, breaking it up into bits.

2. Stir in the tomatoes and spinach and cook for 1 minute, or until the spinach is wilted.

3. Stir in the olive and beaten eggs and scramble the mixture. Cook for 2 minutes, or until the eggs are set to a desired consistency.

4. Transfer the scramble onto a plate and arrange the sliced avocado over it. Sprinkle the cilantro and feta on top and serve immediately.

Cheesy Tofu Quiche

Ingredients:

- 8 oz extra firm tofu, drained and rinsed
- 1 vegetarian mini pie crust
- 1 onion, diced
- 1 garlic clove, minced
- 2 ½ Tbsp. non-dairy milk
- 2 cups spinach, rinsed and dried
- ½ cup Cheddar cheese
- ¼ cup Swiss cheese
- ¼ tsp sea salt

Directions:

1. Set the oven to 350 degrees F.
2. Blend the tofu and milk in a food processor. Season with salt and pepper.
3. Combine the cheeses, onion, spinach, garlic, and milk-tofu mixture in a bowl. Pour into the pie crust.
4. Bake for 15 minutes, or until heated through.
5. Set on a cooling rack for 5 minutes. Slice and serve.

Breakfast Jalapeno Tofu Mix

Ingredients:

- 8 oz extra firm tofu, drained and rinsed
- ½ jalapeno pepper, minced
- ½ bell pepper, minced
- 1 yellow onion, minced
- 1 tomato, diced
- ½ zucchini, chopped
- ¼ tsp. cumin
- ¼ tsp. turmeric
- 1 Tbsp. nutritional yeast
- Sea salt
- Freshly ground black pepper
- ½ Tbsp. olive oil

Directions:

1. Heat olive oil in skillet over medium flame. Sauté onion, garlic, and bell pepper until tender.
2. Crumble tofu into a bowl, and then add into the skillet. Sauté to mix.
3. Add the spices, nutritional yeast, zucchini, tomato, and jalapeno pepper. Sauté until golden and heated through.
4. Season to taste with salt and pepper.

Mushroom Soup with Red Wine

Ingredients:

- 2 shallots, finely chopped
- 1 garlic clove, crushed
- 1/4 lb Portobello mushrooms
- 1 oz dried porcini, soaked in warm water for 30 minutes
- 1 oz dried morels, soaked in warm water for 30 minutes
- 1/4 lb cultivated button mushrooms
- 1/4 cup flat leaf parsley, finely chopped
- 1/2 tsp. fresh thyme, finely chopped
- 1/2 tsp. unsalted butter
- 2 cups vegetable broth
- Pinch of salt
- Pinch of black pepper
- 1/6 cup dry red wine
- 1/6 cup heavy cream
- 1/2 Tbsp. olive oil

Directions:

1. Drain the water from the porcini and morels, reserving the water. Drain the water through a cheesecloth to remove any sediments and set aside.
2. Rinse the Portobello and button mushrooms under cold water. Pat dry, then chop.
3. Place a pot over medium high flame and heat the olive oil and butter. Sauté the shallots, garlic, thyme, and parsley for 2 minutes, then stir in the Portobello and button mushrooms.
4. Stir in the porcini and morels, then add the wine and set heat to high. Once the wine starts to steam, stir in the

broth and reserved water. Bring to a boil, then season with salt and pepper and set heat to medium.

5. Let it simmer for 7 minutes, or until mushrooms become tender.

6. Transfer half of the solids into a food processor and puree until smooth. Pour back into the pot and heat through. Stir in the cream and cook for 3 minutes, or until thickened.

7. To serve, ladle into soup bowls and serve.

Pita Chicken Burger

Ingredients:

- 1 pita, sliced in half
- 2 egg whites, lightly beaten
- 1 cup lettuce, shredded
- 1 pound ground chicken
- ½ cup tomato, diced
- 2 tsp. lemon rind, grated, divided
- ½ tsp. ground black pepper
- ½ cup plain low-fat yogurt
- 1 Tbsp. Greek seasoning mixture
- 1/3 cup breadcrumbs, Italian-seasoned
- ½ cup green onions, chopped
- 1 ½ tsp. fresh oregano, chopped
- 1 tsp. olive oil

Directions:

1. Mix the last 6 ingredients and then add a teaspoon of rind. Stir well.
2. Divide the resulting mixture into 8 equal portions. Shape each into a ¼ thick circular patties.
3. In a big nonstick skillet, heat oil over medium-high head. Place in the patties and allow to cook for about 2 minutes or until browned on each side. Cover and lessen heat to medium and allow to cook for about 2 minutes.
4. Combine the remaining teaspoon of rind, oregano and yogurt. Stir well and fill each pita slice with 1 chicken patty, tomato, lettuce, and yogurt mixture.

Green Beans Salad in Red Wine Vinegar

Ingredients:

- 1/2 lb green beans, trimmed
- 1 oz Spanish ham, chopped
- 1 white onion, minced
- 1 roasted red pepper in brine, diced
- 1 egg, hard-boiled, chopped finely
- 1/6 cup flat leaf parsley, chopped

For the Dressing

- 1 1/2 Tbsp. red wine vinegar
- Fine sea salt
- Freshly ground black pepper
- 1/8 cup extra virgin olive oil

Directions:

1. Steam the green beans for 6 minutes, or blanch them in salted water for 6 minutes. Drain and rinse under cold running water. Drain well or pat dry and set aside.
2. In a bowl, combine the vinegar and olive oil. Season with a bit of salt and pepper to taste.
3. Put the steamed green beans in a serving bowl. Toss in the minced onion, ham, egg, parsley, and peppers. Drizzle the dressing on top, toss, and serve immediately.

Olives and Cheese

Ingredients:

- 1 cup pitted olives
- ½ cup feta cheese, diced
- 2 garlic cloves, sliced
- 1 lemon juice and zest
- 1 tsp. fresh rosemary, chopped
- 2 Tbsp. extra virgin oil
- Freshly ground pepper

Directions:

1. In a medium-sized bowl, combine all the ingredients.
2. Cover and store in the refrigerator for up to 1 day.

Berry and Maple Pancakes

Ingredients:

- ¼ cup berries
- 1 ½ Tbsp. maple syrup
- ½ Tbsp. baking powder
- ½ cup whole wheat flour
- ½ cup non-dairy milk
- 1 Tbsp. olive oil
- 1/8 tsp. sea salt

Directions:

1. Combine the flour, baking powder, and salt in a bowl.
2. Combine the milk, maple syrup, and canola oil in another bowl.
3. Mix the milk mixture into the flour mixture until just combined. Fold in the berries.
4. Heat a non-stick skillet over medium high flame. Ladle the batter into the skillet and cook for 2 minutes per side, or until golden. Repeat with the remaining batter.
5. Stack on a plate and serve.

Paprika Eggs

Ingredients:

- 4 eggs, hard-boiled, sliced
- ½ tsp. salt
- ½ tsp. paprika
- 1 tsp. extra-virgin olive oil

Directions:

1. Sprinkle eggs with paprika and salt.
2. Dip in olive oil. Serve.

Sardines and Greens Salad

Ingredients:

- 2 whole sardine fillets in oil, drained
- 2 sardine fillets in olive oil, drained, chopped
- 2 tomatoes, seeded, diced
- 1 cucumber, diced
- 1/2 red onion, chopped finely
- 1/4 cup flat leaf parsley, chopped
- 1/2 bunch arugula

For the Dressing:

- Fine sea salt
- Freshly ground black pepper
- 1/8 cup extra virgin olive oil
- 1/2 Tbsp. fresh lemon juice

Directions:

1. Toss together all of the vegetables, herbs, and chopped sardines in a salad bowl. Arrange the whole sardine fillets on top.

2. In a small bowl, combine the lemon juice and olive oil, then lightly season with salt and pepper to taste. Drizzle the dressing on top of the salad and serve immediately.

Mediterranean Muesli

Ingredients:

- 3/4 cup oats
- 2 cups low-fat milk
- 1/8 cup raisins
- 1/2 cup puffed rice cereal
- 1/8 cup dried apricots, chopped
- 1/8 cup sunflower seeds, unsalted
- 1/8 cup walnuts
- 2 Tbsp. honey
- 1/4 tsp. cinnamon

Directions:

1. In a mixing bowl, combine the puffed rice cereal and oats with the sunflower seeds, walnuts, raisins and apricots. Add cinnamon or cardamom and stir to combine.

2. Pour the muesli into two separate bowls and add honey and milk. Stir to combine well. Cover with a plastic wrap or lid and refrigerate overnight.

3. The next morning, stir with a spoon. Serve.

Vegetarian Morning Crepes

Ingredients:

- ½ cup whole wheat flour
- 2 ½ Tbsp. non-dairy butter
- 2 ½ Tbsp. non-dairy milk
- 1 Tbsp. maple syrup
- ¼ tsp. stevia
- ¼ tsp. sea salt
- 2 ½ Tbsp. water

Directions:

1. Combine all the ingredients in a bowl. Refrigerate for 2 hours.
2. Place a non-stick crepe griddle over high flame. Reduce to medium flame once hot.
3. Spoon three tablespoons of batter onto the hot griddle. Cook until set. Transfer to a plate and serve with fresh fruit and cream.

Eggplant and Garlic Salad

Ingredients:

- 1 eggplant
- 1 Tbsp. red wine vinegar
- 1 Tbsp. flat leaf parsley, chopped finely
- 3 garlic cloves, minced
- 1 Tbsp. olive oil
- Greek bread

Directions:

1. Set the oven to 350 degrees F. Put the eggplant on a baking sheet; do not slice open.
2. Bake for 30 minutes, or until extremely tender and wilted, turning the eggplant once every 10 minutes.
3. Take the eggplant out of the oven and set aside until cool enough to handle. Then, peel the skin off and slice in half lengthwise to remove the seeds.
4. Chop the eggplant flesh and place into a bowl. Stir in the garlic and parsley, then the vinegar and olive oil. Mix well.
5. Cover the bowl and refrigerate for at least 2 hours. Serve with the Greek bread.

Pumpkin Dark Choco Muffins

Ingredients:

- 7.5 oz pureed pumpkin
- 1/3 cup dark chocolate chips
- ¾ cup whole wheat flour
- ½ tsp. baking soda
- ½ Tbsp. baking powder
- ½ tsp. cinnamon
- ¼ tsp. stevia
- ¼ tsp. sea salt
- ¼ tsp. nutmeg
- 2 ½ Tbsp. water

Directions:

1. Set the oven to 375 degrees F.
2. Combine the dry ingredients, except the chocolate chips, in a bowl.
3. Combine the wet ingredients in another bowl.
4. Mix the wet ingredients into the dry ingredients. Fold in the chocolate chips.
5. Divide the mixture into six muffin tins, silicone or lined with paper liners.
6. Bake for 15 to 18 minutes, or until puffed and set. Cool before serving.

Pumpkin Cilantro Soup

Ingredients:

- 1/2 Tbsp. olive oil
- 1 white onion, diced
- 1/2 tsp. ground nutmeg
- 1/2 tsp. paprika
- 1 cup milk, nut-based preferred
- 1 1/2 cups pumpkin, cooked
- 2 cups chicken broth, low sodium
- 1/8 cup fresh cilantro, minced, divided
- 1/8 cup pine nuts, chopped
- sea salt
- Freshly ground black pepper

Directions:

1. Place a soup pot over medium flame and heat the oil. Stir in the onion and cook for 1 minute, or until translucent. Stir in the paprika and nutmeg, then season with a dash of salt and pepper. Sauté for 1 minute.

2. Stir in the milk and pumpkin. Mix well, then stir in the broth. Let it simmer, uncovered, for 7 minutes, stirring frequently.

3. Turn off the heat and set aside to cool slightly. Transfer the solids and half a cup of soup into a food processor or blender and puree. Return into the pot and stir to combine. Season with salt and pepper to taste, if needed.

4. Stir half of the cilantro into the soup, then ladle into soup bowls and sprinkle the remaining cilantro and pine nuts on top. Serve immediately.

Chapter Five

Lunch Recipes

Moroccan Tomato Soup

Ingredients:

- 4 ripe tomatoes, chopped
- 1/2 tsp. fresh ginger, chopped finely
- 1 yellow onion, chopped
- 1 cup chicken broth
- 1 Tbsp. cilantro, chopped
- 1 1/2 Tbsp. flat leaf parsley, chopped
- 1/2 Tbsp. fresh lemon juice
- 1/2 tsp. paprika
- 1/2 tsp. ground cumin
- 1/2 cinnamon stick
- 1/2 tsp. honey
- 1 Tbsp. extra virgin olive oil

Directions:

1. Puree the tomatoes in a food processor, then set aside.
2. Place a soup pot over medium flame and heat the oil. Sauté the onion for 7 minutes, or until translucent. Stir in the ginger, paprika, cinnamon, and cumin.
3. Add the pureed tomatoes, broth, honey, cilantro, and half of the parsley into the pot. Set heat to medium high and bring to a boil, then set heat to low.
4. Partially cover and let it simmer for 15 minutes, or until a bit thickened. Turn off the heat, let it stand to room temperature, then chill for 3 hours.
5. Ladle into soup bowls and top with the reserved parsley. Serve chilled.

Grilled Salmon with Avocado Salsa

Ingredients:

- 2 salmon steaks
- 1 jalapeno, minced
- Pinch of salt
- 3 Tbsp. red onion, minced
- Pinch of ground black pepper
- 1 garlic clove, minced
- 1 lemon, cut into wedges
- 1 avocado, diced
- 3 Tbsp. flat leaf parsley, chopped finely
- 1 grapefruit, segmented, chopped
- 1 orange, segmented, chopped
- 3 Tbsp. olive oil

Directions:

1. Mix together the olive oil, garlic, parsley, and lemon zest. Add salt and pepper and toss. Place salmon steak into the marinade and set aside for 15 minutes.

2. In the meantime, place the grill on medium-high heat.

3. In a bowl, toss the orange, grapefruit, jalapeno, avocado, parsley and red onion. Season with salt and pepper and toss gently.

4. Grill the marinated salmon stakes for 4 minutes per side or until pink on the inside. Transfer on a serving plate and spoon salsa on the side. Serve immediately.

Green Lentils and Mixed Vegetables Soup

Ingredients:

- ¾ cup green lentils
- 1 onion, diced
- 2 garlic cloves, minced
- 8 oz diced tomatoes
- 1 celery stalk, sliced
- 1 sweet potato, diced
- 1 carrot, sliced
- 2 ½ Tbsp. fresh cilantro, chopped
- Sea salt
- Freshly ground black pepper
- ½ Tbsp. Italian herb seasoning
- 1 tsp. paprika
- 1 ½ Tbsp. olive oil
- 2 ½ cups water

Directions:

1. Place a soup pot over medium flame and heat through. Once hot, add the oil and swirl to coat.
2. Add the onion, carrot, celery, and sweet potatoes. Sauté until tender. Add the garlic and sauté until fragrant.
3. Pour the water into the pot, then add the lentils, tomatoes, paprika, and Italian herb seasoning. Bring to a boil, then reduce to a simmer.
4. Cover and let simmer for 25 minutes.
5. Add the cilantro and stir well. Simmer for an additional 10 minutes, then season to taste with salt and pepper.
6. Serve right away or pack for lunch on-the-go.

Okra in Red Wine Vinegar

Ingredients:

- 1 lb okra
- 1/4 cup onion, chopped
- 1 garlic clove, chopped
- 1/4 cup red wine vinegar
- 1/4 tsp. sea salt
- 1/8 tsp. freshly ground black pepper
- 4 cups water, divided
- 1/2 tsp. sugar
- 1/2 Tbsp. tomato paste
- 2 Tbsp. olive oil

Directions:

1. Place okra in a saucepan and add the 3/4 cup water and the 1/4 cup red wine vinegar. Place over high flame and bring to a boil.
2. Once boiling, set heat to medium, then cover and cook for about 8 minutes.
3. Turn off the heat and take the okra out of the pot using a slotted spoon. Set aside on a plate lined with paper towels.
4. Meanwhile, place a skillet over medium flame and heat the olive oil. Sauté the the onion and garlic until the onion is translucent. Stir in the drained okra.
5. Combine the tomato paste with the 1/2 cup of water, then mix in the sugar, salt, and pepper. Stir the mixture into the pot.

6. Increase the heat and bring to a boil. Once boiling, reduce heat to a simmer, then cover and cook for 25 to 30 minutes. Serve hot.

Lamb Saffron Stew

Ingredients:

- 1/2 lb lamb stew meat
- 1 onion, diced
- 2 tomatoes, pureed
- 1/4 tsp. saffron threads
- 1/2 tsp. ground ginger
- 1/2 tsp. ground turmeric
- 2 cups beef stock, low sodium preferred
- 1/2 cup celery, diced
- 1/8 cup fresh mint, divided
- 1 Tbsp. apple cider vinegar
- 1 1/2 Tbsp. olive oil
- 1 Tbsp. lemon juice
- 1/2 lemon, sliced into wedges

Directions:

1. Place a soup pot over medium flame and heat the oil. Stir in the meat, turmeric, saffron, and ginger, then season with salt and pepper.
2. Cook for 5 minutes, or until the meat is slightly browned
3. Stir in the celery and onion and sauté for 3 minutes, or until the onion is translucent. Add the pureed tomato and beef broth. Stir to combine.
4. Cook, uncovered, for 30 minutes. At the end of the cooking time, use a slotted spoon to take the meat out of the pot and place into a bowl.
5. Puree the soup with an immersion blender or in a food processor or blender.

6. Return the soup and meat into the pot and place over medium flame to simmer, uncovered, for 8 minutes or until thickened.

7. Stir in the lemon juice, vinegar, and half the mint. Mix well, adding seasonings to taste, if needed.

8. Ladle the soup and meat into soup bowls and top with the reserved mint and lemon wedges.

Tuna, Tomato, and Red Pepper Tortilla

Ingredients:

- 1 can light tuna in brine, flaked
- 1 ripe plum tomato, diced
- 1 roasted sweet red pepper in brine, chopped
- 1/4 cup onion, chopped
- 2 eggs
- 1 tsp. dried tarragon
- Pinch of salt
- Pinch of black pepper
- 1 Tbsp. extra virgin olive oil

Directions:

1. Place a nonstick pan over medium heat and add 1/2 tablespoon olive oil.
2. Sauté the onion until transparent then add pepper, tomatoes, tarragon, and tuna. Stir well.
3. Place heat on low and cook for 5 minutes. Remove the pan from heat and set aside.
4. Break eggs into a bowl and add salt and pepper. Beat well. Add sautéed tuna and veggies into the eggs.
5. Clean the nonstick pan and then place over high heat. Add 1/2 tablespoon olive oil and pour in egg and tuna mixture.
6. Place heat on medium and spread the egg across the pan to cook evenly. Flip over once base is cooked. Cook each side for 2 to 3 minutes.
7. Remove from pan and serve.

Grilled Pita with Chickpea

Ingredients:

- 1 can chickpeas, drained
- 1/2 cup flat-leaf parsley, chopped finely
- 1 lemon, zested, juiced
- 1 cucumber, diced
- 3 pita breads
- Pinch of salt
- Pinch of ground black pepper
- 3 Tbsp. olive oil

Directions:

1. In a salad bowl, combine the olive oil, lemon zest, lemon juice, cucumber, chickpeas and parsley. Season with salt and pepper and stir to coat.
2. Place a griddle over medium-high heat and toast the pita bread for 2 minutes per side or until slightly brown.
3. Divide the salad between two plates and place a toasted pita on the side.

Lamb in Tomato Sauce and White Wine

Ingredients:

- 1 lb lamb shoulder, sliced into bite-sized pieces
- 1 tomato, minced
- 1 1/2 oz dry Greek white wine
- 1 garlic, minced
- 1/2 cup yellow onion, chopped
- 1/2 tsp. salt
- 1/4 tsp. pepper
- 1 1/2 oz dry Greek white wine
- 1 bay leaf
- 1/4 tsp. nutmeg
- 1/4 cup tomato paste
- 1 cup water
- 2 Tbsp. olive oil

Directions:

1. Rinse and blot dry the lamb pieces, then set aside.
2. Place a pot over medium flame and heat the olive oil. Saute the onion and garlic until onion becomes transparent.
3. Add the lamb pieces and saute for 15 minutes, or until browned all over.
4. Stir in the wine, nutmeg, salt, pepper, bay leaf, and chopped tomatoes. Cover and cook for 15 minutes.
5. Meanwhile, combine the tomato paste and water in a small bowl and stir into the mixture.
6. Set heat to low and cook for 45 minutes to an hour, or until the lamb meat is extremely tender.

7. Remove the bay leaf, then serve.

Duck Legs with Chickpeas and Olives

Ingredients:

- 2 Duck legs
- 1/2 cup chickpeas, cooked
- 1/2 cup olives
- 6 cilantro sprigs
- 1 yellow onion, thinly sliced
- 1 red bell pepper, sliced thinly
- 1/2 tsp. saffron threads
- 1/4 cup garlic cloves, minced
- 2 Tbsp. fresh ginger, grated
- 1/2 cinnamon stick
- 1 cup chicken broth, low sodium
- 1 bay leaf
- 2 Tbsp. lemon juice, freshly squeezed
- 2 Tbsp. fresh cilantro, chopped
- Pinch of sea salt
- 1/2 Tbsp. extra-virgin olive oil

Directions:

1. Set the oven to 450 degrees F to preheat.
2. Season duck legs with sea salt.
3. Place a heavy-bottomed skillet over medium high flame and coat the inside with oil. Once hot, add the duck legs with the skin-side facing down. Cook for 5 minutes per side, or until golden brown.
4. Take the cooked meat out and set aside on a plate.

5. Stir the onion, garlic, ginger, and pepper into the pot and set heat to low. Stir for 5 minutes, or until the onion becomes translucent.

6. Season with salt, then stir in the cinnamon stick and saffron. Cook until fragrant, then stir in the broth or water.

7. Increase heat to a boil, then scrape the bottom to loosen any browned bits. Transfer the mixture into a tagine, if using. Otherwise, keep cooking in the same pot.

8. Add the duck eggs, then the lemon juice. Let simmer, then cover and cook for half an hour, or until the duck legs are extremely tender.

Curry Squash and Apple Soup

Ingredients:

- 1 lb butternut squash, peeled
- 2 apples, diced
- 1 onion, diced
- 1 ½ tsp. ginger, grated
- ¾ tsp. curry powder
- 1 Tbsp. olive oil
- 3 cups vegetable broth
- ½ tsp. cumin
- 1 cup non-dairy milk
- Sea salt
- Freshly ground black pepper

Directions:

1. Set the oven to 375 degrees F.
2. Cut out a sheet of aluminum foil that is big enough to wrap the butternut squash. Once wrapped, bake for 30 minutes.
3. Remove the wrapped butternut squash from the oven and set aside to cool.
4. Once cooled, remove the aluminum foil, remove the seeds, and peel.
5. Dice the butternut squash, then place in a food processor. Add a non-dairy milk. Blend until smooth. Transfer to a bowl and set aside.
6. Place a soup pot over medium flame and heat through. Once hot, add the olive oil and swirl to coat.

7. Sauté the onion until tender, then add the diced apple, spices, and broth. Bring to a boil. Once boiling, reduce to a simmer and let simmer for about 8 minutes.

8. Turn off the heat and let cool slightly. Once cooled, pour the mixture into the food processor and blend until smooth.

9. Pour the pureed apple mixture back into the pot, then stir in the butternut squash mixture. Mix well, then reheat to a simmer over medium flame.

10. Season to taste with salt and pepper. Serve right away or pack for lunch on-the-go.

Arugula, Cherry Tomatoes, and Artichoke Salad

Ingredients:

- 4 cups arugula
- 1/2 cup cherry tomatoes, halved
- 1/4 cup pomegranate seeds
- 1/4 red onion, diced
- 7 oz canned artichoke hearts, drained

For the Dressing

- 1 tsp. lime juice
- 1 tsp. lemon juice
- 1 Tbsp. orange juice
- Fine sea salt
- Freshly ground black pepper
- 3 Tbsp. extra virgin olive oil

Directions:

1. In a salad bowl, toss together the arugula, artichoke hearts, tomatoes, onion, and pomegranate seeds.
2. In a separate bowl, mix together the orange, lime, and lemon juices and olive oil. Season with a bit of sea salt and black pepper to taste.
3. Drizzle the dressing all over the salad and toss gently to coat. Chill or serve immediately.

Octopus with Frisée and Capers

Ingredients:

- 2 lbs. frozen octopus, defrosted
- 2 roasted red peppers, chopped
- 2 bunches frisée, trimmed
- 1 Tbsp. capers, drained
- 1 garlic clove, thinly sliced
- 2 1/2 Tbsp. red wine vinegar
- 1/2 tsp. dried oregano
- 1/2 Tbsp. oregano, minced
- 2 scallions, white part only, sliced thinly
- 1/2 Tbsp. flat-leaf parsley, minced
- 1 bay leaf
- 1/4 tsp. whole black peppercorns
- 1 1/2 Tbsp. extra virgin olive oil

Directions:

1. To clean the octopus, cut just beneath its eyes and remove the hood. Throw away. Remove and discard the beak and mouth.
2. Place the octopus in a heavy-duty pot over high heat and cover. Let boil and reduce heat to low. Cook for 50 minutes until it becomes tender and turns bright pink.
3. Remove octopus from pot and set aside to cool. Remove purple membrane, if preferred.
4. Slice into 8 tentacles. Slice tentacles into slanted 1/2" oval slices. Place into a large clean jar glass container with a lid.

5. In a mixing bowl, combine the vinegar with olive oil, dried oregano, garlic, peppercorns, and bay leaf. Whisk thoroughly.

6. Pour marinade into the glass jar with the octopus slices and cover. Marinate for 24 hours to 7 days inside the refrigerator.

7. To make the salad, prepare a large bowl and toss the scallions and roasted peppers in it.

8. Spoon the octopus from the marinade using a slotted spoon and transfer into the salad bowl. Add the parsley, oregano and extra virgin olive oil. Stir to combine.

9. Divide the frisee among three plates and spoon the salad over leaves.

10. Drizzle in some more extra virgin olive oil and sprinkle the capers on top.

Roasted Stuffed Snapper

Ingredients:

- 1 whole snapper, gutted
- 4 garlic cloves, chopped
- 2 sun-dried tomatoes, chopped
- 1 cup cilantro, chopped
- 1 cup flat leaf parsley, chopped
- 2 Tbsp. lemon juice, freshly squeezed
- 1 1/2 tablespoons ground cumin seeds
- 3/4 tsp. chili
- 1/2 Tbsp. Spanish paprika
- 1/2 lemon
- Pinch of sea salt
- 2 Tbsp. extra virgin olive oil

Directions:

1. Combine the herbs, tomatoes, paprika, cumin, chili, and lemon juice in a food processor. Pulse until combined, then season with salt to taste. Pulse to a paste.
2. Drizzle in the olive oil as you pulse until everything is thoroughly combined.
3. Set the oven to 425 degrees F to preheat. Line a baking sheet with parchment paper and set aside.
4. Remove the fins from the fish and slice slits on both sides. Rub olive oil all over the fish, then season with salt.
5. Stuff some of the herb mixture into the slits, then stuff the remaining into the fish's cavity.
6. Roast the fish for half an hour, or until cooked through.

7. Place the fish on a platter and squeeze lemon juice from the lemon half. Drizzle some more olive oil on top. Serve.

Ground Beef and Tomato Stuffed Eggplant

Ingredients:

- 2 eggplants
- 3/4 lb. ground beef
- 1 onion, minced
- 2 garlic cloves, minced
- 1/2 tsp. ground cinnamon
- 1/2 tsp. chili flakes
- 1 tsp. ground whole cloves
- 1/2 tsp. ground cardamom pods
- 1 tsp. sugar
- 1 1/2 cups crushed tomatoes
- 1/4 cup fried pine nuts
- 2 Tbsp. fresh flat leaf parsley, chopped
- Olive oil
- Pinch of sea salt
- 1/2 tsp. ground black peppercorns

Directions:

1. Set the oven to 425 degrees F to preheat.
2. Cut slits on one side of the eggplant; be careful not to cut through. Arrange the eggplants on a baking dish, cut sides facing upward.
3. Coat the eggplants with olive oil and sprinkle salt all over. Bake for 20 minutes, or until skin is browned and meat is tender. Remove from the oven and set aside.
4. Place a skillet over medium flame and heat 1/2 tablespoon of olive oil. Saute the onion and garlic until onion is translucent. \Stir in the ground meat and spices. Cook until meat is crumbled and browned all over.

5. Stir in the crushed tomatoes, pine nuts, sugar, and sea salt.

6. Set oven to 350 degrees F. Stuff the eggplants with the meat mixture, then cover the baking dish with aluminum foil.

7. Bake for 25 to 30 minutes, or until eggplant is extremely tender. Top with parsley and pine nuts, then serve.

Chickpea and Brown Rice Patties with Salsa

Ingredients:

- 10 oz canned chickpeas, rinsed and drained thoroughly
- ½ Tbsp. chickpea flour
- 1 cup brown rice, cooked
- 1 egg
- 2 green onions, minced
- 1 garlic clove, minced
- 2 Tbsp. fresh cilantro, minced
- 1 ½ Tbsp. freshly squeezed lemon juice
- 1 ½ Tbsp. ginger, grated
- 1 tsp. curry powder
- 1 tsp. garam masala
- 1 tsp. ground coriander
- 1 tsp. cumin
- ½ tsp. red chili flakes
- olive oil
- ½ tsp. fine sea salt

For the Salsa:

- 1 Tbsp. extra virgin olive oil
- 1 red onion, diced
- ¼ tsp. red chili flakes
- ¼ tsp. lime juice, freshly squeezed
- Fine sea salt
- Freshly ground black pepper

Direction:

1. First make the salsa by combining all of the ingredients for it in a bowl. Mix well, then cover and refrigerate until ready to serve.

2. To make the chickpea patties, combine the brown rice and chickpeas in a food processor. Process until grainy; do not puree.

3. Transfer the mixture into a bowl and add the egg, flour, green onion, cilantro, garlic, ginger, lemon juice, salt, and spices. Mix well with clean hands.

4. Divide the mixture into four patties, then place on a platter and refrigerate for at least 30 minutes to overnight.

5. To cook, place a non-stick skillet over high flame and heat through. Once hot, add the oil and swirl to coat.

6. Add the patties and cook for about 5 minutes per side, flipping only once, or until golden and crisp all over.

7. Spoon the salsa next to the patties. Serve right away or pack for lunch on-the-go.

Chapter Six

Snacks

Feta Nibbles with Poppy Seeds

Ingredients:

- ½ cup feta cheese, crumbled
- 4 sheets filo dough, frozen, thawed
- 1 garlic clove, minced
- 1 Tbsp. poppy seeds
- 2 leeks, white and green sections, thinly sliced
- 1/4 cup melted butter
- 1/4 tsp. brown sugar
- 1/2 cup chicken stock
- 1 bay leaf
- 1 Tbsp. fresh oregano, finely chopped
- 1 Tbsp. olive oil
- Pinch of salt
- Pinch of ground black pepper

Directions:

1. Preheat oven to 400 degrees F. Line a baking sheet with parchment pepper.

2. Place a skillet over medium heat and pour in the olive oil. Sauté the garlic, leeks and sugar for 4 minutes.

3. Add the chicken broth and bay leaf, then season with salt and pepper. Let simmer for 10 minutes or until leeks tenderize and broth evaporates. Remove bay leaf. Set aside to cool.

4. Pour the leek mixture into a bowl and add oregano and feta. Toss to combine

5. Spread out a filo dough on a clean counter and slice lengthwise into three pieces. Brush each piece with melted butter, then put a spoonful of the leek mixture across one end.

6. Fold up that corner to create a triangle and cover the filling. Fold once more until you get a triangular piece.

7. Place on the prepared baking sheet and brush additional melted butter on top. Sprinkle with poppy or sesame seeds, then bake for 20 minutes or until they turn golden brown.

Cabbage and Cheese Sandwich

Ingredients:

- 1 ½ cups cabbage, shredded
- 1 onion, sliced thinly
- 1 green bell pepper, minced
- 2 tsp. lemon juice, freshly squeezed
- 2 tsp. Thousand Island dressing
- 4 slices rye bread
- 2 slices cheese
- 2 tsp. olive oil

Directions:

1. Place a skillet over medium high flame and heat through. Once hot, add the oil and swirl to coat.
2. Add the cabbage, green bell pepper, onion, and freshly squeezed lemon juice. Sauté until cabbage is wilted. Add water, if needed.
3. Spread the Thousand Island dressing on the rye bread and place the cheese on top. Divide the hot cabbage mixture over the open-faced sandwiches, then close the sandwiches with the other rye bread slice.
4. Serve right away or pack for lunch on-the-go.

Gingerbread Waffles

Ingredients:

- 1 egg
- 1/2 cup almond meal
- 1/2 Tbsp. baking powder
- 1 tsp. ground ginger
- 1/2 cup vanilla whey protein powder
- 1/8 cup Splenda
- 1/4 cup heavy cream
- 1/4 cup water
- 1/4 tsp. salt
- 2 Tbsp. butter, melted

Directions:

1. Heat the waffle iron.
2. In a bowl, mix together the dry ingredients. Combine the cream and water in a glass measuring cup and then add the water and egg.
3. Add melted butter and mix well. Add this to the dry ingredients and stir to combine.
4. Pour some of the batter into the waffle iron and bake according to the manufacturer's instructions. Serve with whipped cream if preferred.

Flax Rice Bran Bread

Ingredients:

- 3/4 cup rice bran
- 3/4 cup flaxseed meal
- 2 cups water
- 4 tsp blackstrap molasses
- 2 cups vital wheat gluten
- 3/4 cup whey protein powder, vanilla flavor
- 2 tsp. salt
- 2 Tbsp. olive oil
- 4 tsp. yeast

Directions:

1. Pour all of the ingredients in a bread machine and process based on manufacturer's instructions.
2. Remove the loaf and set aside to cool.

Avocado and Carrot Muffins

Ingredients:

Wet Ingredients

- 3 eggs
- ½ tsp. lemon zest
- ¼ cup honey

Dry Ingredients

- ¼ cup coconut flour
- ¼ tsp. baking powder
- ¼ cup ripe avocado, mashed
- 1/3 cup carrot, grated

Directions:

1. Preheat the oven to 375 °F. Grease and line the muffin tin.
2. Beat the eggs in a large - sized bowl before adding the mashed avocado, carrot, and honey and lemon zest.
3. In a large mixing bowl, sift the coconut flour and baking powder
4. While stirring, mix the wet ingredients with the dry. You'll get a runny batter
5. Pour or spoon the muffin's batter into the cups of the greased muffin tray. Make sure it's not so full, to allow for growth.
6. Bake for 12-15 minutes.

Cold Beans and Olives Salad

Ingredients:

- 1/4 red bell pepper, chopped
- 1/4 green bell pepper, chopped
- 1/2 cup Great Northern Beans, cooked
- 1/2 Tbsp. red wine vinegar
- 2 Tbsp. Kalamata olives, chopped
- 2 Tbsp. fresh dill, chopped
- Pinch of sea salt
- Freshly ground black pepper
- 2 Tbsp. extra virgin olive oil

Directions:

1. To make the salad, toss together the beans, bell peppers, olives, and dill in a bowl.
2. Whisk the vinegar and olive oil together, then drizzle on top of the salad. Toss to coat, then cover the bowl and refrigerate for a minimum of 2 hours. Serve cold.

Peaches and Cream Muffins

Ingredients:

- 3/4 cup frozen peaches, thawed, diced
- 2 eggs
- 1/2 cup sour cream
- 1/2 cup soy flour
- 1/4 cup melted butter
- 1/2 tsp. baking powder
- 1/2 cup vanilla protein powder
- 1/4 tsp. salt
- 1/4 tsp. baking soda
- 1 Tbsp. stevia
- 1 Tbsp. cream
- 1 tsp. orange peel

Directions:

1. Preheat oven to 350º F (180 º C).
2. In a mixing bowl, combine the dry ingredients in a small bowl.
3. In a separate bowl, combine the butter, cream, sour cream, egg, and orange peel.
4. Add the peaches to the dry ingredients then combine the dry with the wet ingredients. Mix until well distributed.
5. Line a muffin tin with paper cups and spoon your batter to fill the tin. Bake for 20 to 25 minutes.

Wheat Lentil Tortillas

Ingredients:

- 2 whole wheat tortillas
- ¼ cup red lentils
- ¾ cup cabbage, shredded
- 1 green onion, chopped
- 1 cup water
- ½ cup bulgur
- ¾ tsp. red pepper flakes
- ½ cup red pepper paste
- 2 ½ Tbsp. tahini
- Pinch of sea salt
- 1 Tbsp. olive oil

Directions:

1. Pour the water into a saucepan and add the lentils. Cover and cook over medium flame for about 15 minutes.
2. Turn off the heat and add the bulgur. Set aside, covered, for half an hour.
3. Meanwhile, place a skillet over medium flame and heat through. Once hot, add the olive oil and swirl to coat.
4. Add the onion, red pepper paste, and red pepper flakes. Sauté until onion is translucent.
5. Pour the onion mixture into the pot of lentil-bulgur mixture. Fold in the scallions and season to taste with salt. Set aside to cool.
6. Spoon the mixture between the tortillas, then add the shredded cabbage and tahini. Roll up securely.
7. Serve right away or pack for lunch on-the-go.

All Vegetables Tacos

Ingredients:

- 4 corn tortilla shells
- 2/3 cup lettuce, shredded
- ½ lb vegetarian sausage, crumbled
- 4 Tbsp. canned black beans, rinsed, drained
- 4 Tbsp. canned corn kernels
- ¼ tsp. chili powder
- 4 Tbsp. salsa
- 1 tsp. lemon juice, freshly squeezed
- 3 Tbsp. cheddar cheese, shredded
- Olive oil

Directions:

1. Combine the corn, beans, cheese, and salsa in a bowl. Set aside.
2. Coat a skillet with the non-stick cooking spray and place over medium flame. Heat through, then add the crumbled vegetarian sausage. Sauté for 1 minute.
3. Add the freshly squeezed lemon juice and chili powder, then sauté for another minute, or until heated through.
4. Divide the crumbled sausage mixture among the tortilla shells, then add the cheesy bean-corn salsa and shredded lettuce. Serve.

Minty Greek Yogurt with Fruits and Nuts

Ingredients:

- 1 cup Greek yogurt
- 2 Tbsp. fresh mint, chopped
- 1 cup purple grapes, halved
- 2 Tbsp. pistachios, chopped
- 2 Tbsp. honey
- 1/4 lemon juice

Directions:

1. Prepare two bowls and divide the 1 cup of Greek yogurt between them.
2. In a separate bowl, mix together the pistachios, grapes, lemon juice and honey.
3. Top the yogurt with the pistachio and grape mix and garnish with mint.

Prosciutto and Figs Wrap

Ingredients:

- 8 figs, halved
- 1.5 oz. prosciutto, sliced thinly
- 16 walnut halves
- 1 Tbsp. honey

Directions:

1. Cut the prosciutto into 16 pieces. Stuff a walnut half for each fig half and then wrap the prosciutto around each piece. Secure with a toothpick if needed.
2. Position the fig bundles and top of a platter and drizzle with honey on top. Enjoy!

Dark Choco Flavored Zucchini Muffins

Ingredients:

Dry

- 3.5 oz dark chocolate, chopped
- 1 cup zucchini, grated
- ¼ cup cocoa powder
- ½ cup almond flour
- 1 Tbsp. tapioca flour
- ¼ cup coconut flour
- 1 tsp. baking soda
- ¼ tsp. salt

Wet

- 4 eggs
- ¼ cup coconut milk
- ¼ cup honey
- ¼ cup ghee, melted
- 1 tbsp. vanilla extract

Directions:

1. Set the oven to 350°F. Grease and line a regular sized muffin pan with paper liners.
2. Beat the eggs in a large - sized bowl and whisk in melted ghee. Pour in the honey, coconut milk and vanilla. Whisk thoroughly to combine well.
3. Get a separate bowl and sift the dry ingredients, the flours, baking soda, cocoa powder and salt.
4. Put the dry ingredients in the large bowl with the wet ones.

5. Stir in the grated zucchini and half of the dark chocolate chunks.

6. Use a spoon to transfer the muffin's batter into the lined muffin cups. Sprinkle the top with the remaining chocolate chunks.

7. Bake in the oven for 25-30 minutes, test if the toothpick comes out clean

8. Remove from oven and. Let the muffins cool for 5 to 10 minutes in the tin before removing the muffins to cool in the rack.

Honey Onion Biscuits

Ingredients:

- 2 onions, roasted
- 3 eggs
- 1 cup almond flour
- 1 tsp. baking soda
- ¼ cup coconut flour
- 1 tsp. honey
- 3 Tbsp. ghee
- 1 tsp. sea salt

Directions:

1. Preheat oven to 325°F.
2. Using a blender or a food processor, puree the onions.
3. Mix the eggs and pulse again.
4. Add the flours, salt and baking soda. Pulse again.
5. Drop in the ghee while the food processor is blending. The batter is supposed to be firm.
6. Scoop 2 tbsp. of batter onto the cookie sheet on a baking pan. Flat the dough to form it into biscuit shape. Do this for the rest of the batter.
7. Smooth out the biscuits by dipping your hand in a bowl of water and run circles over the biscuits.
8. Bake for about 22-25 minutes until they turn slightly brown.
9. Remove from oven. Let cool before serving.

Butter Pecan Munchies

Ingredients:

- 1 egg
- 1/2 stick butter
- 1/2 cup pecans, chopped
- 1/2 Tbsp. molasses
- 1/8 cup oat flour
- 1/8 cup almond meal
- 1/4 tsp. vanilla
- 1/2 cup Splenda

Directions:

1. Preheat oven to 325 degrees F (170 degrees C).
2. Place the butter in a microwaveable bowl and melt it in the microwave on 40 percent power for 1 minute.
3. Add the molasses, Splenda, eggs, and vanilla. Stir to combine. Add the almond meal and oat or low-carb flour. Stir to combine. Add the pecans and stir to distribute evenly.
4. Grease a baking pan or mini-muffin pan with oil and transfer the batter into it. Bake for 25 minutes.

Blueberry Pie

Ingredients:

- 2 cups frozen blueberries
- 4 Tbsp. butter
- 1 1/4 tsp. baking powder
- 1/4 cup almond meal
- 1/8 cup Splenda
- 1/4 cup heavy cream
- 1/2 Tbsp. lemon juice
- 1 tsp. salt

Directions:

1. Preheat oven to 275 degrees F (190 degrees C). Grease a baking pan and set aside.
2. In a bowl, mix the blueberries together with 1/8 cup Splenda, and lemon juice. Toss to coat and transfer into the pan. Distribute evenly. Spoon two 1/2 tablespoons of butter.
3. In a bowl, mix together the almond meal, 1/2 tablespoon Splenda, baking powder, and salt.
4. Melt 3 tablespoons of butter and combine with the cream in a bowl. Add this to the dry ingredients stir well until thoroughly mixed.
5. Pour the batter over the blueberries in the pan, making sure it is even. Bake for 30 minutes or until the crust is golden brown. Serve warm.

Butter and Soy Pecans

Ingredients:

- 2 Tbsp. butter, melted
- 1 cup shelled pecans
- 1/2 tsp. ground ginger
- 1 1/2 Tbsp. soy sauce

Directions:

1. Preheat oven to 300 degrees F (148 degrees C).
2. Strew the pecans across a shallow roasting pan. Add the butter and stir to coat. Roast for 15 minutes.
3. Remove from heat and add the soy sauce. Stir to coat.
4. Sprinkle the ginger on top and stir to coat as well.
5. Roast for 10 more minutes. Set aside to cool before serving.

Veggie Burrito Wheat Wrap

Ingredients:

- 2 whole wheat tortillas
- 2 tsp. chipotle pepper in adobo sauce, minced
- ½ cup diced tomatoes
- ½ cup corn kernels
- 1 cup wild rice, cooked
- 1 avocado, pitted, diced
- 2 tsp. cumin
- 1 cup cheddar cheese, shredded
- 6 Tbsp. salsa
- 2/3 cup canned black beans, rinsed
- ½ cup fresh cilantro leaves, torn
- 4 Tbsp. lime juice, freshly squeezed
- Pinch of sea salt
- Pinch of ground black pepper

Directions:

1. Combine the corn, cilantro, avocado, black beans, and lime juice in a bowl. Season with salt and pepper.
2. In another bowl, combine the rice, chipotle peppers, cumin, and salsa.
3. Spread the rice mixture on the tortillas, then add the black bean mixture on top; do not include the liquids.
4. Top with tomatoes and cheese, then roll up securely.
5. Place a grill pan over medium flame and heat through. Place the wraps on the hot grill and grill for 2 minutes or until lightly toasted. Serve.

Chapter Seven

Dinner

Italian Tuna Fillets with Raisins

Ingredients:

- 2 tuna fillets
- 1 Tbsp. capers in brine, drained
- 1 1/2 Tbsp. olive oil
- 1/4 cup red onion, minced
- 1/8 cup white wine vinegar
- 1/3 cup celery, minced
- 1 Tbsp. golden raisins, soaked in 1 1/2 Tbsp. warm water
- Pinch of salt
- Pinch of black pepper

Directions:

1. Lightly season the fillets with salt and pepper.

2. Place a skillet over medium high flame and heat half of the olive oil. Cook one fillet for 3 minutes per side, turning once.

3. Transfer the fillets onto a platter, cover, and set aside. Repeat with the second fillet.

4. Heat the remaining oil in the skillet over medium flame and sauté the onion and celery until tender.

5. Stir in the capers and raisins together with the soaking water. Let simmer until the water evaporates.

6. Place the steaks over the mixture and add the vinegar. Cover and cook for 3 minutes, or until the fish is very tender. Adjust seasonings if needed. Serve immediately.

Cheesy and Creamy Cauliflower Salad

Ingredients:

- 1/2 head cauliflower
- 4 oz. cream cheese
- 1/8 cup mayonnaise
- 8 oz sour cream
- 1/4 cup onion
- 1/4 tsp garlic powder
- 1/4 tsp. salt
- 1/4 tsp. pepper
- 1 cup cheddar cheese, shredded

Directions:

1. Slice the cauliflower into bite sized florets. Rinse and drain thoroughly.
2. In a mixing bowl, mix the mayonnaise and cream cheese with an electric beater until smooth.
3. Add sour cream, garlic powder, salt, and pepper. Mix well.
4. In a separate bowl, mix together the cauliflower, onion, and shredded cheddar. Pour the dressing over the cauliflower and fold to combine. Serve.

Shrimp and Tomato Pasta

Ingredients:

- 1/4 lb. linguine pasta
- 1/2 lb. Roma tomatoes, chopped
- 3/4 lb. shrimp, peeled and deveined, heads and tails removed
- 1 garlic clove, minced
- 1/4 cup basil leaves, chopped
- 1/8 tsp. red pepper flakes, crushed
- Pinch of salt
- Pinch of ground black pepper
- 1/2 Tbsp. olive oil

Directions:

1. Cook the pasta according to the manufacturer's instructions using a large sauce pan. Once it is done, drain it and set aside in the sauce pan.
2. Meanwhile, place a large skillet over medium heat and pour in the olive oil. Sauté the garlic for a minute.
3. Add the crushed red pepper flakes, tomatoes, and basil. Let simmer for 12 minutes.
4. Stir in shrimp and allow to simmer for 4 minutes or until the shrimp is cooked through. Remove the shrimp and place on a plate and set aside.
5. Add the sauce to the cooked pasta and shrimp in the saucepan. Season with salt and pepper, then toss. Serve.

Honey Chicken Glaze

Ingredients:

- 2 chicken breasts, boneless, skinless
- 1/4 cup chicken broth, low sodium
- 1 tsp. honey
- 2 cloves garlic, slivered
- 1/4 cup pureed tomatoes
- 1 Tbsp. olive oil
- 1/2 cup yellow onion, thinly sliced
- 2 Tbsp. balsamic vinegar
- Pinch of salt
- Pinch of black pepper

Directions:

1. Season the chicken with salt and pepper.
2. Place a skillet over high flame and heat the oil. Brown the chicken, then set aside. Save a tablespoon of fat in the skillet.
3. Set heat to low and sauté the onion and garlic until wilted. Stir in the tomato puree and broth, scraping the bottom to loosen any chicken bits.
4. Put the chicken back into the skillet. Cover and let simmer for 15 minutes, or until tender. Set on a platter and cover to keep warm.
5. In a bowl, combine the vinegar and honey, then pour into the skillet. Stir for 4 minutes, or until thickened. Drizzle on top of the chicken and serve.

Kelp Curry Noodles

Ingredients:

- 2 cups raw kelp noodles, rinsed
- ½ cup red bell pepper, julienned
- 1 cup bean sprouts
- ½ cup fresh Thai basil leaves, torn
- 2/3 cup watermelon radish, julienned
- ½ cup fresh cilantro leaves, torn
- ½ cup carrot, julienned
- ½ cup zucchini, julienned
- ½ cup celery, diced
- 1 avocado, pitted
- ½ cup raw cashews
- 2 tsp. sesame seeds
- 2 tsp. sesame oil
- 2 Tbsp. lime juice, freshly squeezed

For the Sauce

- 1 ripe avocado, peeled
- 2 tsp lemongrass, chopped
- 1 tsp ginger, chopped
- ½ cup carrot juice, freshly squeezed
- Pinch of sea salt
- Pinch of ground black pepper
- 1 tsp green curry paste

Directions:

1. Combine all of the ingredients for the curry sauce in a blender. Blend until smooth and creamy. Set aside.

2. Toss together the julienned vegetables, sesame oil, cilantro, basil, bean sprouts, and lime juice in a bowl.

3. Divide the kelp noodles between two bowls. Divide the vegetable mixture between the two servings, then spoon the curry sauce on the side; do not drench the vegetables.

4. Halve the avocado, remove the pit and scoop out the flesh. Slice thinly and place on top of the servings. Add the watermelon radish and season with sesame seeds and cashews. Serve.

Teriyaki Chicken Salad

Ingredients:

- 3/4 lb chicken breast, boneless
- 2 cups iceberg lettuce, chopped
- 2 cups chopped leaf lettuce
- 3/4 cup red cabbage, chopped
- 1/6 cup canned pineapple chunks in juice, diced
- 1/4 cup salsa
- 3 Tbsp. Teriyaki sauce
- Lime and Mustard Dressing

Lime and Mustard Dressing

- 1/8 cup Dijon mustard
- 1/8 cup Splenda
- 3/4 Tbsp. maple syrup
- 3/4 Tbsp. canola oil
- 3/4 Tbsp. cider vinegar
- 3/4 Tbsp. lime juice

Teriyaki Sauce

- 1/4 cup soy sauce
- 1/8 cup dry sherry
- 1 garlic clove, crushed
- 1 Tbsp. Splenda
- 1/2 Tbsp. ginger root, grated

Directions:

1. For the honey lime and mustard dressing, in a bowl, whisk all of the ingredients together.

2. For the Teriyaki sauce, mix all of the ingredients together in a bowl.

3. For the grilled chicken salad, marinate the chicken in the Teriyaki sauce inside the refrigerator for at least 2 hours and preferably overnight.

4. In a salad bowl, combine the iceberg and leaf lettuces, red cabbage, and pineapple bits

5. Prepare your chicken for grilling by draining the marinade into a bowl and grilling the chicken, basting it with the marinade. Cook on both sides for 3 to 5 minutes or until well done. Slice cooked chicken into pieces.

6. Toss the salad with the Lime and Mustard Dressing. Distribute salad between two plates and top with sliced grilled chicken. Spoon salsa on top of the chicken and serve.

Lamb and Beef Meatballs

Ingredients:

- 1/8 lb ground lamb
- 1 lb ground beef
- 1 egg, beaten
- 1/2 tbsp. garlic, chopped
- onion, minced
- 1/2 Tbsp. dried oregano
- 1/2 Tbsp. fresh mint, chopped
- 1/2 Tbsp. fresh mint, chopped
- 1/3 cup unseasoned dried breadcrumbs
- 1/2 tsp. sea salt
- 1/4 tsp. ground black pepper
- Olive oil

Directions:

1. Mix together the ground meat with the onion, egg, mint, oregano, garlic, mint, bread crumbs, salt, and pepper using your hands.
2. Cover the bowl and refrigerate for at least 30 minutes.
3. Take the mixture out and divide into 6 to 8 even meatballs.
4. Set the broiler on high to preheat, then coat the pan with olive oil. Put the meatballs into the pan and broil for 8 to 10 minutes.
5. Flip the meatballs over and broil for an additional 8 or 10 minutes. Serve hot.

Garlic Broccoli

Ingredients:

- 1 broccoli head, chopped into florets
- 1 garlic clove, minced
- ¼ tsp. freshly squeezed lemon juice
- 1 ½ Tbsp. olive oil
- Pinch of sea salt
- Pinch of ground black pepper

Directions:

1. Set the oven to 400 degrees F.
2. Spread the chopped broccoli on a baking sheet. Drizzle the olive oil and season to taste with salt and pepper. Toss well to coat.
3. Sprinkle with freshly squeezed lemon juice.
4. Roast for 15 minutes.
5. Best served warm.

Shrimp with Romesco Sauce

Ingredients:

For the shrimp

- 8 shrimp, peeled, deveined
- 1/2 Tbsp. olive oil
- 1/2 lemon, sliced into wedges
- Pinch of sea salt

For the Romesco Sauce

- 1/4 cup yellow onion, chopped
- 2 garlic cloves, minced
- 1 ripe tomato, chopped, juices retained
- 1/2 Tbsp. extra virgin olive oil
- 1 roasted bell pepper in brine, drained, chopped
- 2 Tbsp. blanched almonds
- 2 Tbsp. hazelnuts
- 1 fresh chili pepper, roasted, peeled, chopped
- 1/2 cup clam juice or fish stock
- 1 Tbsp. red wine vinegar
- 2 Tbsp. dry white wine
- Pinch of salt
- Pinch of ground black pepper

Directions:

1. To cook the sauce: Place a large, heavy-duty skillet over medium heat. Pour in the olive oil and allow to heat up.
2. Sauté the onions for 5 minutes or until translucent. Add the garlic, chili, and roasted bell pepper. Stir to combine.

Add the tomatoes. Cook for 5 minutes or until the tomato juices evaporate. Add the wine and stock.

3. Cover and place heat on medium-low to simmer. Cook for 30 minutes.

4. Meanwhile, place a dry skillet over low heat and toast the hazelnuts and almonds. Turn off the heat and let cool.

5. Pour into a food processor and grind until mealy and chunky. Add sherry or red wine vinegar and pulse to mix.

6. Remove the tomato sauce from the heat and set aside to cool, then pour it into the food processor with the nut mixture. Pulse to combine. Season with salt and pepper and set aside.

7. Place a non-stick skillet over medium-high heat. Add olive oil and tilt to evenly distribute. Increase heat to high and place shrimp into the skillet. Sear for 4 minutes or until bright pink.

8. Flip shrimp and sear on the other side. Season with sea salt and serve with Romesco sauce and lemon wedges.

Red Peppers Stuffed Rice and Mushrooms

Ingredients:

- 2 ¼ cups wild rice, cooked
- 1 ½ cups shiitake mushrooms, chopped
- 3 garlic cloves, chopped
- 6 red bell peppers
- 1/3 tsp. turmeric
- ¾ cup pine nuts
- ¾ cup vegetable broth
- 1/3 tsp. all spice
- 1 tsp. fine sea salt
- 4 Tbsp. olive oil

Directions:

1. Set the oven to 375 degrees F.
2. Place a large skillet over medium flame and heat through. Once hot, add 3 ½ tablespoons of olive oil and swirl to coat.
3. Add the garlic and sauté until fragrant, then stir in the mushrooms, pine nuts, spices, and salt. Sauté until the pine nuts become lightly toasted.
4. Add the broth and stir well to combine. Add the cooked wild rice and fold well to combine. Cook, stirring occasionally, until the rice has completely absorbed the broth. Remove from heat and set aside.
5. Lightly coat a baking dish with the remaining olive oil.
6. Slice the tops of the bell peppers off, taking care to preserve the "lids." Scoop out the seeds and discard.

7. Stuff the bell peppers with the wild rice mixture, then arrange in the prepared baking dish. Place their tops over them.

8. Bake for 20 minutes, or until the bell peppers' skins are lightly blistered and tender.

9. Serve right away or pack for lunch on-the-go.

Baked Aioli Fish Fillets

Ingredients:

- 4 white fish fillets
- 4 Tbsp. Aioli
- 2 Tbsp. Parmesan cheese, grated

Aioli

- 1/2 egg, beaten
- 1 garlic clove, crushed
- 1/2 Tbsp. lemon juice
- 1/8 tsp. salt
- 1/4 cup olive oil

Directions:

1. Preheat oven to 350 degrees F.
2. To make the Aioli: Place the egg, salt, lemon juice, and garlic in a blender. Blend to combine while gradually pouring the oil into it. Once the sauce becomes thick, turn off the blender.
3. Grease a baking pan and place the fillets in it. Spread the Aioli on the fillets and top with Parmesan cheese. Turn and spread some more Aioli and sprinkle more Parmesan.
4. Bake for 20 minutes and serve.

Greek All Veggie Salad

Ingredients:

- 1 onion, finely chopped
- 2 garlic cloves, minced
- 1 ripe tomato, grated
- 1 eggplant, cut into ¼-inch rounds
- 1 green pepper, seeded and cut into strips
- 2 zucchini, cut into ¼-inch rounds
- 1 potato, peeled, sliced into ¼-inch rounds
- Pinch of sea salt
- Pinch of ground black pepper
- Olive oil

Directions:

1. Season eggplant, zucchini and pepper with salt in three separate colanders,. Set aside to drain for 1 hour. Wipe dry.

2. Place a large skillet over medium heat and pour 1/4 inch of olive oil. Deep fry onion and garlic for 6 minutes, then remove with a slotted spoon and set aside. Add potato and sauté until edges become crisp.

3. Prepare a large, wide pot and pour 1/4 cup olive oil into it.

4. After potatoes are cooked, remove from the skillet with a slotted spoon and transfer into the pot. Add salt and pepper, then add a third of the onion and garlic mixture on top.

5. Lightly fry the zucchini in the same skillet until lightly colored, then remove with a slotted spoon and transfer

to the top of the potatoes in the pot. Add a third of the onion and garlic mixture.

6. Lightly fry the eggplant slices and also transfer with a slotted spoon on top of the zucchini in the pot. Add a third of the onion and garlic mixture.

7. Lightly fry the pepper to soften then place on top of the eggplant layer. Add black pepper, followed by the grated tomato.

8. Cover the pot and let simmer over low-medium heat for 20 minutes until vegetables become tender. Spoon into salad bowls and enjoy!

Bake Meatballs Stew

Ingredients:

- 2 1/2 lb ground lamb
- 3 eggs
- 1 cup chickpeas, cooked
- 4 garlic cloves, minced
- 1/2 onion, diced
- 2 cups tomatoes, crushed
- 4 oz tomato paste
- 1 1/2 Tbsp. sea salt
- 1 1/2 Tbsp. ground caraway seeds, toasted
- 1 red bell pepper, diced
- 1/2 tsp. sugar
- 1 Tbsp. olive oil
- 2 Tbsp. fresh cilantro, chopped

Directions:

1. In a bowl, combine the ground meat with the tomato paste, caraway seeds, and sea salt. Mix well, then refrigerate for at least 2 hours (can be refrigerated up to 12 hours).
2. To make the sauce, place a saucepan over medium flame and heat the oil. Stir in the onion, garlic, and bell peppers.
3. Season with salt, then cook until onion is translucent and peppers are tender.
4. Stir in the crushed tomatoes, then cook for 15 minutes, or until turned into thick sauce. Stir in the sugar and chickpeas, then the remaining salt.

5. Cook until thoroughly combined, then turn off the heat and set aside.

6. Set the oven to 350 degrees F to preheat. Take the meat mixture out of the refrigerator and divide into small balls using a spoon.

7. Place an ovenproof skillet over medium flame and heat the canola oil. Add the meatballs and cook until browned all over.

8. Pour some of the sauce into the saucepan until half an inch high. Crack the eggs into the skillet, on top of the sauce; take care not to break the yolks.

9. Transfer the skillet into the oven and bake for 8 minutes, or until the eggs are set to your desired doneness. Take out of the oven, sprinkle cilantro on top, then serve.

Chapter Eight

Desserts

Cinnamon Sweet Potato Biscuits

Ingredients:

- 1 ½ cups pureed sweet potato
- 3 cups whole wheat flour
- 1 ¼ tsp. ground cinnamon
- 3 tsp. baking powder
- ¾ tsp. ground ginger
- 2/3 cup milk
- ½ cup butter
- 1 tsp. stevia
- 2/3 tsp. sea salt

Directions:

1. Set the oven to 400 degrees F. line a baking sheet with parchment paper.
2. Combine the dry ingredients in a bowl.

3. Cut the butter into the dry ingredients until the mixture looks crumbly.

4. Combine the pureed sweet potato with the milk in another bowl. Mix this into the dry ingredients.

5. Transfer the dough onto a lightly floured surface and knead well. Roll out with a rolling pin until ¾ inch thick. Cut into 24 pieces and arrange on the baking sheet, an inch apart.

6. Bake for 15 minutes, or until golden brown. Let cool at room temperature.

Honey Chives Biscuits

Ingredients:

- ¼ cup chives, chopped
- 2 tsp. honey
- 1 tsp. baking soda
- 3 Tbsp. ghee
- ¼ cup coconut flour
- 3 eggs
- 1 cup almond flour
- 1 tsp. sea salt

Direction:

1. Preheat oven to 325°F.
2. Using a blender or a food processor, puree the chives. Or simply chop them finely.
3. Mix the eggs and pulse again.
4. Add the flours, salt and baking soda. Pulse again.
5. Drop in the ghee while the food processor is blending. The batter is supposed to be firm.
6. Scoop 2 Tbsp of batter onto the cookie sheet on an aluminum baking pan. Flat the dough to form it into biscuit shape. Do this for the rest of the batter.
7. Smooth out the biscuits by dipping your hand in a bow of water and run circles over the biscuits.
8. Bake for about 22-25 minutes until they turn slightly brown.
9. Remove from oven and let cool before serving.

Apple and Cranberry Crumble

Ingredients:

- 4 1/2 Tbsp. whole wheat pastry flour
- 5 sweet apples, sliced thinly
- 5 tart apples, sliced thinly
- 2/3 cup cranberries
- 1 1/2 tsp. orange peel
- 1/6 tsp. ground cloves
- 1/3 tsp. nutmeg
- 1 1/2 tsp. cinnamon
- 3 Tbsp. maple syrup
- 1 1/2 cups apple cider
- 3 Tbsp. vegan margarine
- 2/3 tsp. sea salt

For the Topping:

- 3 Tbsp. whole wheat pastry flour
- 1 1/2 cups rolled oats
- 1 1/2 cups raw pecans
- 3/4 cup coconut flakes, unsweetened
- 2/3 tsp. sea salt
- 2/3 tsp. cinnamon

Directions:

1. Set the oven to 350°F. Lightly grease a baking dish and set aside.

2. Mix together all of the ingredients in a large saucepan, except the vegan margarine and the ingredients for the topping. Place over medium high flame and cook for 5 minutes.

3. Transfer the mixture into the prepared baking dish and dot the vegan margarine on top. Set aside.

4. In a food processor, mix together all of the ingredients for the topping. Process until thoroughly chopped up. Spread over the apple mixture evenly.

5. Bake the apple crumble for 30 minutes.

6. Before serving, place on a cooling rack for 5 minutes. Best served with vegan ice cream.

Brown Rice, Almonds, and Raisins Pudding

Ingredients:

- 1 ¾ cups brown rice, cooked
- ¼ tsp. cardamom
- ¼ cup raisins
- ¼ cup toasted almonds, chopped
- ½ cup non-dairy milk
- ½ tsp. cinnamon
- 2 ½ Tbsp. maple syrup

Directions:

1. Combine all the ingredients in a saucepan. Place over high flame and bring to a boil.
2. Once boiling, reduce to low flame. Simmer for 5 minutes. Serve right away.

Cinnamon Dark Choco Oatmeal Bars

Ingredients:

- 1 1/2 cups rolled oats
- 1 1/2 cups ground rolled oats
- 1 1/2 tsp. cinnamon
- 1/2 cup dark chocolate chips
- 1 1/2 Tbsp. ground flax seeds
- 1 1/2 cups coconut sugar
- 1/2 cup coconut oil, unrefined
- 1 1/2 cups almond flour
- 2/3 tsp. baking soda
- 4 1/2 Tbsp. water
- 1 1/2 tsp. vanilla extract

Directions:

1. Set the oven to 350°F to preheat. Line a baking pan with parchment paper and set aside.
2. In a bowl, combine the water and flax seeds. Set aside to thicken for 5 minutes.
3. In a separate bowl, combine the coconut oil and sugar. Beat using an electric beater, then beat in the thickened flax seeds and vanilla extract, followed by the salt, cinnamon, and baking soda.
4. Beat in the remaining dry ingredients until thoroughly mixed.
5. Transfer the mixture into the prepared baking pan, packing tightly, then scatter the chocolate chips evenly on top.

6. Bake for 20 minutes, then set on a wire rack to cool before you slice and serve. Store in an airtight container and refrigerate for up to 1 week.

Cheesy Olives and Rosemary Topping

Ingredients:

- 1/2 cup Kalamata olives, pitted, sliced
- 1/2 tsp. fresh rosemary, chopped
- 1/4 cup feta cheese, diced
- 1 garlic clove, sliced
- ½ lemon juice and zest
- 1 Tbsp. extra virgin olive oil
- Pinch of ground black pepper
- Dash of red pepper flakes, crushed

Directions:

1. In a bowl, mix together the feta, olives, crushed red pepper flakes, black pepper, lemon juice and zest and olive oil.

2. Serve with crackers or whole wheat bread. Consume within 24 hours.

Banana Oats Muffins

Ingredients:

- 1 banana, mashed
- ½ cup rolled oats
- 1 tsp. baking soda
- ¾ cup spelt flour
- ½ tsp. cinnamon
- ¼ cup maple syrup
- ¼ cup olive oil

Directions:

1. Set the oven to 375 degrees F.
2. Combine the dry ingredients in a bowl.
3. Combine the wet ingredients in another bowl
4. Mix the wet ingredients into the dry ingredients.
5. Divide the mixture into six muffin tins, silicone or lined with paper liners.
6. Bake for 15 to 18 minutes, or until puffed and set. Cool before serving.

Almond and Apricot Cookies

Ingredients:

- 3 eggs, beaten
- 5 cups blanched almond flour
- 1 1/2 cups slivered almonds
- 1/3 cup dried apricots, sliced into slivers
- 1 1/2 tsp. lemon zest, grated
- 1 1/2 cups honey
- 1 1/2 tsp. vanilla extract

Directions:

1. Preheat the oven to 300 degrees F. Prepare a baking sheet by lining it with parchment paper.
2. In a mixing bowl, combine the almond flour, vanilla, lemon zest, and honey. Mix well, then slowly stir in the beaten eggs until well incorporated.
3. Knead the mixture using your hands until it forms into a paste. Divide the dough into 28 balls and set aside.
4. Chop the slivered almonds and spread them on a plate. Roll each ball of dough across the almonds to coat.
5. Arrange the balls on the lined baking sheet and press a sliver of dried apricot over each ball.
6. Bake for 12 minutes, or until golden brown. Set on a wire rack to cool for at least 8 minutes before serving.

Almond and Cacao Bites

Ingredients:

- 2 Tbsp. cacao nibs
- 1 cup whole almonds, roasted
- 1/2 tsp. corn starch
- 2 Tbsp. brown sugar
- 1/2 tbsp. maple syrup
- Pinch of sea salt
- 1/2 tsp. warm water
- 1/2 tsp. pure vanilla extract

Directions:

1. Set the oven to 325°F to preheat. Cover a rimmed baking sheet with baking paper and set aside.
2. In a coffee grinder, combine the sugar, cacao nibs, and salt. Grind until fine.
3. Combine the warm water and cornstarch in a glass bowl until the corn starch is completely dissolved. Add the maple syrup and vanilla extract, then stir to mix.
4. Place the almonds into the mixture and turn to coat.
5. Stir the cacao mixture into the bowl with the almonds until evenly combined.
6. Spread the coated almonds on the prepared baking sheet, then place in the oven and toast for 7 minutes.
7. Carefully shake the baking sheet to disturb the almonds, then toast again for about 3 to 4 minutes, or until the coated almonds look more dry.

8. Set the baking sheet on a cooling rack and allow to cool completely.

9. Once cooled, transfer into an airtight container and refrigerate for up to 14 days. Divide into five servings in separate containers.

Dates and Walnuts Nibbles

Ingredients:

- 1/2 cup dates, finely chopped
- 2 1/2 Tbsp. cocoa powder
- 2 1/2 Tbsp. dark chocolate chips
- 2 1/2 Tbsp. walnuts, chopped
- 2 1/2 Tbsp. sesame seeds
- 1/4 tsp. vanilla extract
- 1/8 tsp. sea salt
- 1/4 tsp. cinnamon

Directions:

1. Combine all the ingredients in a food processor or blender and pulse until it becomes a thick paste.
2. With a tablespoon, scoop out the paste and form into balls. Arrange the balls on a tray that could fit inside your freezer.
3. Once the entire mixture has been divided into balls, freeze them for at least 20 minutes. Serve chilled and store any excess in a covered container in the freezer for up to 2 weeks.

Conclusion

I hope this book was able to help you better understand the Mediterranean diet and the many numerous health benefits that it can provide.

This not-so-restrictive diet has been evaluated to possess all important nutrients for best health. According to research, the Mediterranean diet scores big for encouraging good heart health and lessens your risk of developing other heart diseases. It likewise reduces your risk for certain types of cancer, cholesterol and blood pressure levels, and other chronic diseases.

The Mediterranean diet is a complete eating and lifestyle strategy that continues to be one of the most excellent recommendations for a longer, healthier life.

The next step is to give the Mediterranean diet a try as well as the many recipes presented in this book. Soon enough, you will start enjoying the benefits offered by this diet.

Armed with the proper knowledge of these important components, it will be much easier for you to plan your meals, lead a healthy lifestyle, and follow the Mediterranean diet for good.

Finally, if you enjoyed this book, please take the time to share your thoughts and post a positive review on Amazon. It'd be greatly appreciated!

www.ingramcontent.com/pod-product-compliance
Lightning Source LLC
Chambersburg PA
CBHW071522080526
44588CB00011B/1528